KW-756-447

The Manual of Frequently applied Tools, Techniques
and Methodologies used
in a
Modern Lean Environment

Tools

For

Success

Part of the
Instant Lean Series

Written by

Barry Jeffrey and Graham Ross

Tools for Success.

Written by Barry Jeffrey and Graham Ross

ISBN   978-1-4452-1989-9

© KaizenTrainer.com 2009

Limit of Liability

About the Authors

Barry Jeffrey

Barry is a Lean Consultant and author with over 20 years experience in managing, teaching and consulting in Lean methodologies.

His main specialities are: Managing Lean transformation programmes; Teaching, developing and coaching Lean leaders; Sensei type consulting ; Lean new production introduction methodology and Training in Lean methodologies

Website: http://www.excolo.co.uk

Graham Ross

Graham is a Lean Consultant and author with over 20 years experience in Operational Improvements. He helps people save Time, Energy, and Money by teaching them about "Lean Thinking".

He specialises in: Managing Public Sector Lean Transformations; Lean Training; Kaizen Blitz interventions and Lean Facilitator Coaching, Training and Development.

Website: http://www.leankaizen.co.uk

Authors' Acknowledgements

The authors would like to acknowledge the help of Helen Marriott and Jan Ross for their support during the creation of this book. They especially assisted with dotting our "I"s and crossing our "T"s.

Contents

Contents

List of Diagrams and Tables

Introduction

Welcome to **_Tools for Success_**, part of the **_Instant Lean_** series.

This book is a handy reference of the processes and tools that surround Lean methodology.

The aim of this book is to provide you with all the information that you require to function in a busy Lean environment, without the complicated explanations that you see in many publications.

Lean is relatively simple, 90% is common sense.

The most difficult part can be knowing when to apply the correct tools.

This book will help you understand the various tools, and where and when you should apply them.

Do not fall into the trap of thinking that Lean applies only in manufacturing environments. In fact, this perception could not be further from the truth. The tools covered in this book work equally well in office situations.

The main principle of Lean is the identification and removal of waste that exists within most processes.

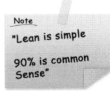

Note

"Lean is simple

90% is common Sense"

Lean is a word that simply describes an organisation or process in which the right things are done well at the right time, with the minimum amount of resources.

How to use this book

This handbook includes a collection of Lean tools that can and should be used in everyday applications.

This book does not focus on theory. It is designed to explain in quick, easy terms, the principles of Lean. It focuses on the key points that are required to make a Lean process work well.

This book will not teach you all aspects of Lean, but it will give you the building blocks and the reminders that we all need from time to time.

Correct application of the tools in this book will help you:

- Understand your place in the big picture

- Identify Waste in the process

- Improve Quality

- Make your workplace visual

- Use standard work effectively

- Understand your level of competence and how to improve

Overview of Lean

The principles

The term Lean and all of its various methodologies are not new. In fact, many of the concepts have been around for over 100 years. The real development of the ideas into an overall system was pioneered by Toyota in the period following the Second World War.

The Toyota Production System (TPS) has been the subject of countless number of studies over the years. Many companies have tried to emulate it. Many have tried to make a science out of the methodologies it employs. Some have even added to its complexity by adding additional tools and techniques to the process. Yet, at the very core of the Toyota Production System, there are two very simple concepts.

"Profit through Cost Reduction"

and

"Make what the customer needs, when they need it, in the quantity that they need".

The ultimate goal of any business is to make profit, and the Toyota Production System is no different. It uses cost reduction through the elimination of various wastes to achieve this.

The House of Lean

The House of Lean is a visualisation to help explain how Lean works. It shows how all of the components of the system must work together, in order for the complete process to be optimised.

The house like any building has:

Foundation   -   Production Smoothing

2 pillars   -   Just in time & Jidoka

And a roof (covering the complete system)

Figure 1.1 House of Lean

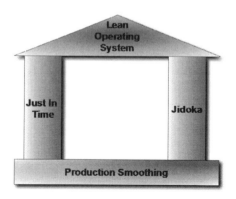

Like with any building if one of the pillars is weak or not there, the roof will collapse.

If the foundation is weak or missing, over time again the building will crumble.

This reminds us, that in the Lean world, we must pay attention to all aspects of the process, not just the ones we understand and find easy.

For definitions of Just In Time (JIT), Jidoka and Production Smoothing see the glossary of term at the back of the book.

Understanding Value Streams

About this section

Value streams and their analysis are very important to help in understanding the problems and the potential for improvement in any process.

A Value stream is the 'journey' of a part or product through the processes from one point to another. Normally this is from the point of customer order to the point where the order is fulfilled.

A Value stream map is a simple visualisation of exactly what is going on at any point in time in a process. The map is used to show Work In Process (WIP) and resource utilisation. If we do not map and understand the entire process, improvements may be sub optimised. Carried out in isolation, there is a real danger that any improvements that are made will not filter through to the customer or improve overall efficiency.

How to apply it

1. The first thing to do is to identify the product you are going to analyse. This can be a single product or indeed a product family, as long as the path through the process is common. The tool not only works on manufactured products, it works equally well on documents and electronic items. Indeed, many of the biggest areas of waste in any business are normally found in the support services where documents are 'held up'. Value stream mapping is ideal for highlighting these problems accurately.

2. Set up a small team to help with the mapping process. Between them, they should have the knowledge of the process steps involved. From suppler to customer.

3. The most important thing to remember is to use live data. Do not rely on systems (since they are often wrong and the source of the problem). Go to the shop floor or the work area and physically walk the process so you can witness what is *actually* happening.

4. Start to draw your Value Stream Map (VSM) working from the customer and working backwards. Use the symbols shown in figure 1.2 on page 16
The best way is to draw the map on a wall covered with lining paper so that the team can all see it. Use cut out symbols and pencils to connect it up, because it is normal to make a few mistakes as you discover what is really going on.

5. Start by outlining the process as you understand it, working from the customer end first. You can modify this as you find out more.

6. Identify the data you need to accumulate e.g.

- Cycle time
- Number of people
- Batch size
- Lead time
- Inventory
- Scrap levels

Figure 1.2 Value Stream Mapping Symbols

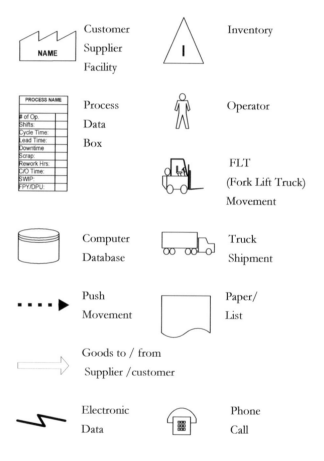

Customer
Supplier
Facility

Inventory

Process
Data
Box

Operator

FLT
(Fork Lift Truck)
Movement

Computer
Database

Truck
Shipment

Push
Movement

Paper/
List

Goods to / from
Supplier /customer

Electronic
Data

Phone
Call

7. Gather the data for each step. Make sure that you capture real data by physically visiting each process and counting and timing. Do not accept peoples' guesses. Once you have the data, complete the data box.

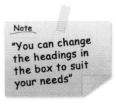

Note

"You can change the headings in the box to suit your needs"

PROCESS NAME	
# of Op.	2
Shifts:	1
Cycle Time:	10s
Lead Time:	100s
Downtime	3%
Scrap:	5%
Rework Hrs:	N/A
C/O Time:	N/A
SWIP:	4

8. Now link it all up using the data flow arrows.

9. Calculate the overall lead time for the complete VSM. This is done by simply looking for the longest cycle time in the process and multiplying by the total process inventory. (this is because all parts must pass through this bottleneck in the process)

10. Now mark up the Value Added Processes. These are the ones that add value by transforming the information/product in someway into what the customer requires e.g. drill a hole, processing a document etc. Remember processes like inspection and washing components are **not** value added. Also remember that when the parts are waiting, this is Non Value Added.

11. Add an overall time line to show the lead time for the item i.e. how long it spends in the whole process. Differentiate between Value Added Time and waiting time by drawing the line as in Figure 1.3, page 19.

12. Calculate the Value Added Ratio by adding up the total Value Added Time and dividing this by the total lead time.

13. This will allow you to see the big picture as it is now. To really see the way forward, now draw a map of your ideal new process. Show all products flowing to customer demand, with a minimum Work In Process. Consider scheduling, and the use of visual management, to make items move as required.

14. Look at the actions required to achieve this new process. List these and apply priorities. This will give you an improvement plan (kaizen action plan), that can be implemented over time.

In conclusion.

Value Stream Mapping helps you:

- See the bigger picture
- Understand the bottlenecks within the process
- Identify waste within the process
- Focus and prioritise improvement activities

Note
"When you start, it is normal to find the Value Added Ratio is less than 1% "

Figure 1.3 Example of a Value Stream Map

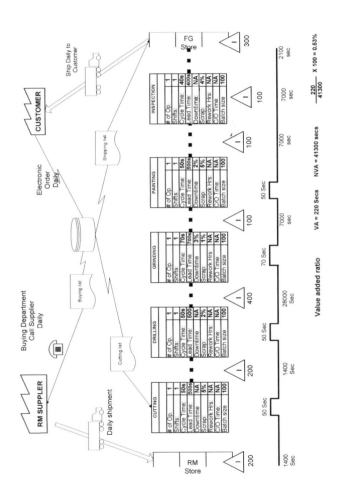

Process Mapping

About this section

Process Mapping is in many ways similar to Value Stream Mapping. The difference being that a process map tends to focus on a specific process, rather than a complete product Value Stream.

It is a way to pinpoint who does what over time in a particular process. It is a method for depicting the process, material or information flow, in a diagrammatic form.

A process map is a powerful method for distinguishing Value Adding and Non Value Adding activities by identifying the key steps in the process.

When should you use it

Process Mapping can be used at any time to gain clarity and understanding of your current condition.

In general process mapping is best used when you want to move from the current state to an improved future state.

Where should you do it

It is best to create your process map physically close to the business process that you are mapping. This allows the process mapping team to 'walk' the process if required to gain further clarity and understanding.

Why use it

The main reason to map a process is to gain information about your current condition, and the current wastes involved, with the view to creating an improved future state.

It helps us understand who does what over time and the 'hand offs' between areas, delays, and bottlenecks.

The process map helps us identify current turnaround times and how they are made up. Mapping the process can also give team members a better knowledge of the activities of other functions involved, out with their areas of expertise. This can lead to a higher level of understanding and improved co-operation between groups.
 i.e. People get a sense of the 'big picture' often for the first time.

How to apply it

1. Set up a small team to help you with the process. To put a representative process map together it is best to use a cross functional multi level team with responsibilities for the processes being reviewed. Team members should have a sound knowledge of their particular part of the business, and the team should have enough breadth of experience to cover all of the business process activities. If there are small areas of very specific knowledge that are gaps, then we should arrange to have experts on standby to come and share their knowledge at the appropriate time. Typically the team should consist of 6 to 10 people and it is always useful to have an experienced facilitator, who is neutral, to lead the activity.

2. You will need to prepare some basic materials ahead of time in order to create your process map. The most common requirements are:

   • Sticky notes

   • Markers

   • Flip chart paper/ Lining paper

   • Sticky tack.

You will need to arrange the use of a large room for the duration of the exercise.

The time required obviously depends on the size of the task, but one day is the suggested maximum for this activity.

3. Start creating the map by joining several pieces of flip chart paper together and attach them to the wall. Experience will tell you how big the backdrop for your process map needs to be. Using flip chart paper allows you to add or take away as required.

4. Make everyone aware of the process mapping symbols. (see figure 1.4). It is best to use the coloured sticky notes to represent the process mapping symbols. You can adapt/draw onto the sticky notes to get the symbol shapes you require. Create a colour key for your process map, which is used consistently by everyone.

5. Discuss the key departments, write them individually on a sticky note and place them on the very left hand side of your process map.

6. Obtain consensus as to the start and end points of the process. This is very important, as lack of agreement at this stage can cause confusion and delays later on. Use the oval symbol to show the start point.

Note

"Map what actually Happens....
Not what you think Happens...."

7. Start to build the map using the symbols going from left to right. Show the dependencies between groups, and continue building until the complete map has been created. Map what actually happens, not what you would like to think happens.

8. Add time scales along the top, so that the overall turnaround time can be estimated.

Figure 1.4 Process Mapping Symbols

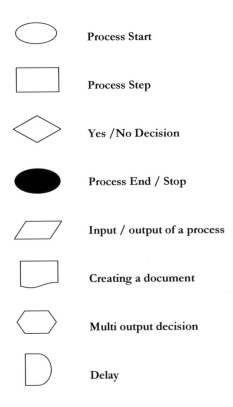

Process Start

Process Step

Yes /No Decision

Process End / Stop

Input / output of a process

Creating a document

Multi output decision

Delay

Figure 1.5 Process Map Example

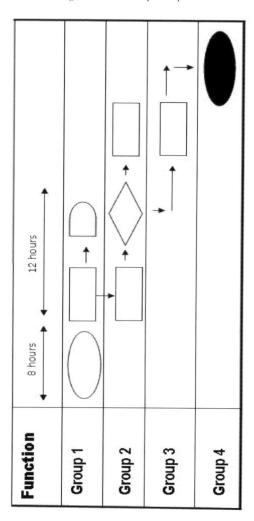

9. The next step is to identify the waste. Once the Map is complete, go through it and identify potential waste in the process. Be very critical at this stage. Do not accept Non Value Added processes as being 'necessary'.

10. Once you have completed identifying the waste, the next step is to draw a 'future state map'. This should be your 'ideal' process with all the waste removed. It may not be possible to achieve this new process straight away. The new map can serve as a target to achieve.

11. The final step is to implement the improvements identified. Make a plan. Things that can be done immediately, and tasks that will require more planning. Ensure that all tasks have an implementation date and an owner.

Top Tip

A good Process Map should have 'swim lanes' to separate the activities of each function.

This can be quickly and easily achieved by folding your flip chart paper or lining paper in a concertina fashion, prior to hanging it on the wall.

Figure 1.6 Example of Flip Chart Folding

Here is an example of the effect that you are trying to achieve

In conclusion

It always amazes team members to witness how much waste is going on, once they start to map their processes.

Process Mapping is a great way to gain a common understanding of the challenges facing a business.

Process Maps can be time consuming, so you should only go to the level of detail required to achieve you improvement objectives.

You should only map the areas where you are trying to make an impact. Avoid the 'Let's map everything' situation; where the information becomes wallpaper with no action taking place as a result of the Mapping Process.

When an individual comments that "I've already mapped this process", be guarded. Some organisations have 'professional' process mappers who create their individual idea of how a process should operate.

Frequently maps are generated to 'comply with a requirement of an approval body for quality or compliance'. Often these 'maps' look pretty but don't actually tell the real story.

It is the act of getting people involved and the sharing of information that makes process mapping powerful.

The task of jointly putting the map together creates a sense of ownership and urgency which cannot be achieved when an individual draws up a 'theoretical' map from the comfort of their desk.

Try it! It may create objectivity to mundane tasks and uncover exciting opportunities.

Process mapping helps you:

- See the bigger picture
- Understand the linkage between different departments
- Understand where the delays occur within the process
- Identify Waste within the process
- Focus and prioritise improvement activities

Spaghetti Diagrams

About this section

The Spaghetti diagram is a very visual way to depict the movement of material, people or information, through a process in a diagrammatic form. Since, in most processes there is a lot of movement, the diagram will look complex, hence the name, Spaghetti diagram, simply because the result typically looks like a bowl of spaghetti.

A Spaghetti diagram helps identify movement waste that is often not even recognised as such. e.g. walking to and from a printer that is located too far from the people using it.

It helps us determine the physical flow and distance that products/information and people travel to process work.

The spaghetti diagram helps us to 'see' processes and procedures in a different way.

When should you use it

The Spaghetti diagram can be used at any time to gain clarity and understanding of your current condition.

In general the Spaghetti diagram is best used when you want to move from your current state to an improved future state.

Where you should use it

The Spaghetti Diagram tool can be applied in both office and shop floor environments. It can also be used to understand movements between suppliers, customers, and production sites. In fact, any situation where 'Non Value Added' movement exists.

Why use it

The main reason to create a spaghetti diagram is to document the current movement of work and people.

It gives us an insight into the distances travelled, and the number and locations that work has to travel to.

It clearly shows transport wastes, and gives us a 20,000 ft view of our operations which we rarely encounter on a day to day basis.

How do you create it

Creating Spaghetti Diagrams can be done in a number of different ways. The choice will depend on the complexity of the process and what type of movement you are observing.

Method A

This method is best used on complex processes and the multi site type of situation when one requires to understand a number of different flows at the same time e.g. Material, people, documents. etc.

1. Set up a small team, normally 3 or 4 people is enough.

2. Prepare the following items ahead of the exercise.

    -   Different coloured sticky notes, markers, flip chart paper
    -   Sticky tack, Sticky tape, small dot labels
    -   A schematic or floor plan of your workplace
    -   Balls of different coloured string.
    -   A room with a large enough space to create the diagram (typically big enough for four to six pieces of flip chart paper joined together)

3. Join several pieces of flip chart paper together and lay them out on the desk. (Experience will tell you how big this needs to be)

4. Draw an outline of the area to be examined, roughly to scale.

5. If possible, walk the process to get a 3 dimensional feel of what is involved and take notes regarding the layout of the current process.

6. The best method is to physically follow the flow. Walk the process following the product/information and person. Record the route that is taken on a small scale map.

7. Create cut outs (to scale) using the sticky notes of the various elements of the work place, and lay them in position on the diagram e.g. equipment, storage, materials etc

8. Once you are happy with their positioning sticky tape the cut outs onto the paper.

9. Decide on a colour key for the various workflows you want to chart (use the different coloured string to represent these)

10. Start to build up the diagram by placing the string at your process start (sticky tack the string down at the start point)

11. Unwind the string until reaching the next step in the process and sticky tack it down. Continue this until the diagram is complete.

12. The reason for using sticky tack is that 9 times out of 10 the team will change their mind about what actually happens.

13. Once you are happy that the string is in the correct position, sticky tape it down.

14. Analyse the diagram and look for opportunities to minimise transport waste. To measure the distances travelled, if you know the scale, measure the string!

Method B

This method is best used for observing processes which are more local to each other, such as on an assembly line. Typically this method is used to observe operator movement between different parts of the process. Normally only one type of flow is recorded at one time e.g. operator movement or material movement.

1. Begin by either drawing or obtaining a layout of the area concerned. Ensure all the key parts of the process are marked. Machines, material, walkways etc. Try to keep you diagram to scale if you are drawing it.

2. Observe the process. As the operator moves around the process draw a line on the map tracing the path taken.

3. This process can be repeated for a number of cycles to ensure that the operator is consistent. Use different colour pens if possible.

4. Once the observation is complete, analyse the results. Measure the distance travelled.

5. Look for ways to reduce the amount of movement by either moving material or processes closer together or perhaps changing the work sequence.

Figure 1.7 Example of a Spaghetti Chart

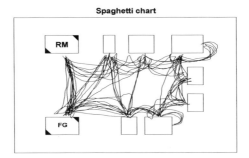

Spaghetti chart

In conclusion

The spaghetti diagram is a great way to identify movement waste.

It provides a real bird's eye view of the process, and can give a great start to identifying layout issues that are creating poor flow, extra travel, and wasted time.

It communicates waste that isn't always obvious, especially to those personnel that aren't involved in doing that particular process.

Remember that every line that has been drawn in the spaghetti diagram is movement waste.

The Seven Classic Wastes

About this section

Waste exists in all parts of every organisation and an ability to identify it is a vitally important part of Lean operations. This section will tell you about the seven classic wastes that exist in most processes.

How to apply it

In order to understand waste in more detail, let's take a look at a man that has been working in your organisation for some time now. He is not a good man. He is a low life.

He has been undermining everything you do with great ease and effectiveness. His work can be seen in just about every area of your business. He is very clever, many people do not even realise what he has been up to.

His plan is to suck the very lifeblood out of your business. He wants to make it a place with little future, where enthusiasm is frowned upon, and blame is easier than praise.

So who is this man? **His name is Tim Wood**.*

Why have you never heard of him before? He is not in your Outlook directory.

OK, **Tim Wood** is not a real person, but he does exist in your organisation. Tim Wood is actually a handy little acronym for the seven classic types of wastes that exist in most businesses.

(* TIM WOODS was originally thought up by Michael G. Moran at Moran3)

The 7 Wastes

T is for Transport Waste

Transportation at any level is waste. In a perfect process, all of the processes would be located next to each other in sequence. So any deviation from this is waste. Movement of paperwork in an office environment is a waste. Movement of material from a stores area to a shop floor is waste, as is its transportation from one department or facility to another.

I is for Inventory Waste

We need to have enough inventory of work in our system to keep things moving along, but not so much that it reduces flow and masks problems. Using 'just in time' we minimise the potential for error, reduce delays and help reduce costs.

M is for Motion Waste

It goes without saying that we need to move our bodies to remain healthy. The waste we are talking about here is 'excess' motion e.g. having to walk to fetch materials or unnecessary key strokes or having to get up and down so someone else can check your work.

W is for Waiting Waste

We need to minimise 'waiting' time. This can be people 'waiting' or material waiting to be processed e.g. waiting for information from someone else; waiting for a computer screen to refresh; waiting for an approval; waiting to use the photocopier or fax machine.

O is for Over Producing Waste

We should always aim to only produce what the next process requires i.e. the previous process should 'pull' work from us, rather than us 'pushing' work onto them. The overall process can only go as fast as the slowest process.

By not over producing we reduce the amount of inventory of work in the pipeline and thus improve turnaround times.

O is for Over Processing Waste

Over processing occurs when we do something unnecessary that is not required by our customers. e.g. putting a document in a plastic wallet, and then putting 10 plastic wallets together with a rubber band, then putting the 10 plastic wallets in a crate to transport to the next department 3 floors away. If the next process was co-located, you could just hand over individual documents one at a time!

D is for Defect Waste

By reducing the number of errors, we reduce the amount of rework, which in turn reduces our costs and our turnaround times.

How often has work flowed through your organisation without stopping for some sort of error?

Very few businesses perform proper analysis of the defects that are preventing flow. Once the chronic few are identified, you need to do something about them.

Now that we have introduced you to Mr **Tim Wood**, you need to start thinking about ways of getting rid of his bad influence on your current operations.

Identifying the Seven Wastes

We have already mentioned that an easy way to remember the seven wastes is by using the handing acronym TIM WOOD.

T	Transport waste
I	Inventory waste
M	Motion waste
W	Waiting waste
O	Over Producing waste
O	Over Processing waste
D	Defects waste

Once you remember the acronym TIM WOOD you will never forget the Seven Wastes.

What most people find difficult is the ability to recognise the different types of wastes in the work place.

Investigate your own workplace and look for examples of the seven different type of waste and write them down.

Once you've identified the seven wastes start to think about ways that you could eliminate them.

In conclusion

Eliminating the Seven Wastes is fundamental to becoming Lean.

If you are serious about Lean it is important to know what the seven wastes are, and develop your ability to recognise them!

'The elimination of these Seven Wastes is fundamental to creating a Lean enterprise.'

5S/ Workplace Organisation

About this section

In this section we will take you though a powerful methodology to help you improve you workplace organisation, called 5S.

What is it

So what is 5S / Workplace Organisation and what is it all about?

5S is a methodology for creating a high performance workplace that is free of clutter and has 'a place for everything and everything in its place'.

It is fundamental to creating a Continuous Improvement Culture. It is the foundation that we build a Lean Organisation upon.

5S is a structured way of implementing excellent workplace organisation that helps us facilitate an efficient working environment that people in the organisation can be proud of.

5S is not just about housekeeping and keeping the place tidy! 5S helps us determine what things are needed and where they are needed.

The 5S technique is intolerant of waste, and helps you create an environment where things are easier to find, and abnormality visually jumps out at you. Adopting 5S improves productivity with fewer errors.

It creates a better working environment which is free of clutter leading to stress reduction for staff.

What are the 5S

The 5S originated from 5 Japanese words but in the west they are generally described as follows:

1. Sort

2. Straighten

3. Scrub

4. Systems

5. Sustain

Different Organisations use different acronyms for explaining the 5S. The table below depicts some of the more popular ones:

Table 1.1   5S Acronyms

Name	5S	Japanese	5C	Cando
Stage 1	Sort	Seiri	Clear Out	Clean up
Stage 2	Straighten	Seiton	Configure	Arranging
Stage 3	Scrub	Seison	Clean & Check	Neatness
Stage 4	Systems	Seiketsu	Conform	Discipline
Stage 5	Sustain	Shitsuke	Custom & practice	Ongoing Improvement

Regardless of which acronyms are used, the process can be broken down into basically 5 distinct stages.

Table 1.2 5S Stages

Stage 1	Separating what is needed from what is not
Stage 2	Organising the way needed things are kept
Stage 3	Ensuring the environment is kept clean and free of clutter
Stage 4	Reviewing the first 3 stages and making improvements on a regular basis
Stage 5	Motivating staff to maintain the process

When to use it

5S is a core fundamental to any Lean programme and should be one of the first disciplines that is put in place. All employees should be trained in the process and encouraged to practice the process daily.

Where to use it

5S should be rolled out across all departments equally. It is not just a shop floor process. Failure to do this will mean that the process will not be treated with respect and the wastes in the processes will be more difficult to find.

Why bother with 5S

Having a well organised, efficient workplace is fundamental to helping you deliver on your Quality, Cost and Delivery goals. Only the fittest organisations will survive during these competitive times.

By applying 5S successfully you can make problems visible and abnormalities jump out. This in turn gives you opportunities to improve processes and eliminate deep seated waste. Making things 'visible' helps you to eliminate errors, defects and injuries.

5S helps you 'wash out the dirt' from your Organisation and give staff a sense of pride in their workplace.

Resistance to Change

If you can create an environment where 5S is accepted as "The way we do things around here", then you are well on the way to creating a vibrant Lean Culture.

There is a strong possibility that before getting to that situation there will be a degree of resistance to 5S and the changes that take place as a result.

"I know where everything is"

"Are you trying to turn us into robots?"

"I keep this stuff because it may come in handy one day"

"If we have shared equipment someone will steal it"

The key to doing 5S well is to start narrow and deep .Perfect a small piece of workplace Organisation before you go onto the next bit.

Once the improvements are sustained then move on, but not before. People need to physically own the changes if you are to be successful.

What is Sort

Sort means, clearly distinguishing between
- What is needed and should be kept?
- What is not needed and should be removed?

"If in doubt move it out"

Take a look around your own work environment. Many of the items are either no longer required, have never been required, or are broken and require repair.

They may have been 'borrowed' from a different department and never returned or are simply in the wrong place or are poorly labelled and identified.

In general this amounts to 'clutter'. This 'clutter' is taking up lots of space, which in turn makes it harder to find the items that you actually need.

Poorly organised space usually leads to the waste of holding excess inventories of items.

To make matters worse you can't find the items that you actually do need.

On average, each person wastes about 1 hour each day searching for items.

The Red Tagging Process

One very practical way to sort out what we need from what we don't need is by conducting a red tagging process.

This involves using conspicuous red tag labels, to attach to objects that should not be in the area or are not in good order.

41

The Main steps are as follows:

1. Inform everyone ahead of time that a red tag campaign will be taking place in the area and that everyone's help will be needed.

2. Identify an area to store red tagged items temporarily.

3. Identify red tag targets and criteria. Typically if something has not been used within a month, then we may choose to red tag that item.

4. It can be useful to do a red tag walk through to create a list of potential red tag targets prior to starting physically red tagging.

5. Attach the red tags to targets and document activity on a log sheet and then move them into the red tag area.

6. Once all items have been red tagged, then the team should review each red tagged item to agree on the appropriate course of action. These may include; reorganising the way items are stored, relocating items, repairing broken items, or disposing of the item if it is no longer required.

Typical Red Tag Targets

- Desks or work benches

- Cabinets

- Files and Folders

- Out of date documents

- Broken Equipment

- Equipment no longer used

- Tools

- Excess inventories or materials

- Paperwork

- Shelves

- Chairs

- Out of date items

However, we must never red tag people!

Once all items have been red tagged, then the team should review each red tagged item to agree on the appropriate course of action.

These may include; reorganising the way items are stored, relocating items, repairing broken items, or disposing of the item if it is no longer required.

By using a Red Tag Strategy as part of the first S stage, Sort, we can separate things we need, from those things we don't need.

Doing the first S can have a big impact. It can free up a lot of space in the workplace.

What is Straighten

Straighten means organising the way needed things are kept, so that anyone can find them easily.

- There must be a location for all needed things.

- There must be a limit to how much of each item can be stored (maximum inventory)

- Make the items easy for anyone to find, use and return.

Implementing the Straighten Phase

The aim is to create an environment where there is a place for everything and everything has a place. A bit like a surgeon's operating theatre or the pit area of a Formula1 Racing Team.

Doing this will help:

- Eliminate searching time (waste)

- Make things easier to get to, and use. Put the most frequently used items nearby.

- Make things easy to put back. Maintain the orderliness.

- Make things understandable at a glance. Use visual controls.

Note

"Make the process Visual so everyone Knows where items are stored.."

The main steps in the Straighten process are:

1. Create a set in order / set in process plan. For every item that is in the workplace we need to plan the following:

   - The type of physical storage / container
   - Quantity of the item to be kept
   - Item placement / location
   - Item label and identification code

Figure 1.8 Example of Re-organisation

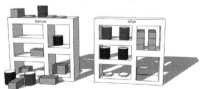

The plan should cover every item and be the basis for a Standard Operating Procedure around Workplace Organisation.

2. Locate items closest to the work station first. Normally this will be tools that are used on an hourly or daily basis. In the case of an office environment the same principles apply; frequently used items should be located on the desk.

3. Shadow boards can be a great way to create visual impact. Basically an outline or shadow is created for the item so that it is easy to see, if it is there or not.

Figure 1.9 Shadow Board

4. Working away from the workstation, the next consideration is normally materials. Whatever method you have planned for storage of materials, design them in such a way as to create a First In, First Out situation (FIFO).This ensures that the inventory of items are used in the correct sequence.

Many organisations use chutes and gravity to help create this inventory flow.

5. Item placement - A general rule of thumb is that items used frequently should be located close by and those items used less frequently further away. For instance in a storage rack, the frequently consumed items should be stored at belly height and less frequently consumed items at the top or bottom depending on weight.
If items are not needed then we should get them 'out of the flow'. Put things where they are needed and create standard locations for equipment and materials.

6. Train good habits - By spending time and effort in making the workplace visual, staff will respect and take pride in the new environment. This in turn should lead to the formation of good habits where people put things back ready for the next time.

   By doing the second S, Straighten well, we can create an environment where abnormality jumps out.

7. Take Pictures - Fixed point photography can be a great way to document the environment once you have implemented the Set in Place Plan.
   By taking pictures and documenting the workplace you can create a visual standard of 'how things should be'.

   This can be a good reminder to staff of the standards we are trying to maintain and improve upon.

What is Scrub

Scrub means, creating a clean work environment that is free from clutter and contamination, and more importantly creating a process to maintain the cleanliness of the area.

Implementing the Scrub Phase

There are various things we need to do to make the third S, Scrub happen.

1. Identify the daily cleaning activities and routine maintenance that will be required to maintain the standard of the area.

2. Try out the cleaning activity and identify any cleaning materials or training that will be required.

3. Calculate how long the process takes. Five to Ten minutes a shift is the ideal. More than this generally means that the scrub process is too complex and will not be sustained.

4. Document daily cleaning activities including who, when and how.

5. Use visual boards to show cleaning activity status.

6. Zone areas to avoid duplication of effort and create ownership.

7. Focus on shared areas of the workplace and make a named individual responsible for them:

- Create standards for maintaining personal workspace.

- Identify and resolve areas of chronic contamination.

- Set up a system of daily walk a rounds to ensure that there are no areas of clutter and take immediate action if there is.

Inspect as you Clean

One of the advantages of cleaning the work environment on a zoned regular basis, is that sources of contamination and faults can be detected early, before they lead to a chronic failure in the system. By identifying sources of dirt, counter measures can be put in place to eliminate them.

Note

"If it doesn't get dirty you don't need to clean it"

Total Productive Maintenance

By implementing the third S, Scrub, you will create an environment that is receptive to using a Total Productive Maintenance System, which is another building block of creating a Lean Culture.

What is Systems

The fourth S, Systems is about regularly reviewing the first 3S's regularly to identify sources of abnormality and make further improvements.
The fourth S is concerned with making the first 3 S's unbreakable.

For instance:

Sort:

Use a few red tags every day in the workplace to avoid clutter building up.

Straighten:

Continually think of ways to make it impossible to put things in the wrong place.

Scrub:

Find the sources of dirt and clutter and develop counter measures.

Implementing the Systems Phase

1. Make someone responsible for maintaining this review system.

2. Create a Standard Operating Procedure for reviewing the first 3S at set intervals.

3. As you review each of the first three S's and find abnormality do the following:

- Ask "why" 5 times until you get to the route cause of the problem, and then apply counter measures.
- Make sure the improvements are implemented professionally and well documented. Ensure all staff are trained in the new way of working.

What is Sustain

Sustain, means creating an environment, where the 5S has been adopted as a way of life. Adopting the fifth S means that people are continually thinking of ways to make things even better.

Once you have created a fantastic workspace, guess what, unless you maintain discipline, then very quickly it will revert back to the old clutter and inefficiency that you had before.

At this point in the 5S process the involvement of management at all levels of the organisation is vitally important and critical to the success of the programme. The senior managers must be seen to 'endorse' the process, being seen to provide resources and time for daily 5S activities to take place.

It's a good idea for the directors to periodically conduct a 5S walk in which they are seen to praise good effort and suggest improvements where the process has slipped a little.

Implementing the Sustain Phase.

Here are the most important activities required to implement the fifth S, Sustain:

- Stick to the rules and procedures you set out

- Audit the workplace on a regular basis and share the results

- Create improvement actions based on audits and follow through on all the actions with the people responsible

- Train all new employees in the 5S

- Create visual story boards with before and after pictures of workplace improvements

- Make 5S a habit for all staff and encourage correct behaviours

- Use check lists and visually display the results

- Use point photographs to maintain standards

- Raise performance expectations around 5S with staff

In conclusion

The 5S process is fundamental to becoming Lean and it is a core building block in any Lean process. Without implementing the basics you will not see abnormalities easily.

5S is difficult to do well, but done correctly it is a very powerful tool. It takes time and effort to make it stick.

Visual Management

About this section

Visual management is another very important part of the Lean system. It allows us to understand the status of the process easily and without effort. It is the process of creating an environment where things are obvious from the minute you walk into the area.

Visual information needs to be relevant, useful, and up to date.

How we present information is only limited to our own imaginations.

Visual Management is often an area that people shy away from. This is because it is very simple in concept but often difficult to execute well.

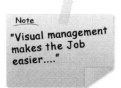

Note

"Visual management makes the Job easier...."

Visual Management is not a new thing

Figure 2.0 Early Andon Example

The famous industrialist Robert Owen introduced the Figure 2.0 idea of a 'silent monitor'. This was to encourage people working in the mills.

The monitor was a small, wooden block which hung next to each person's machine. The colour facing out showed how well things were going.

The status was indicated by the colour of the side:

- White = excellent
- Yellow = good
- Blue = indifferent
- Black = bad

As Robert Owen walked through the mills he could immediately see the issue areas on the shop floor, without talking to anyone.

When and where to use Visual Management

Visual management is a tool that can be used in all parts of a business from the boardroom to the smallest department.

The trick is to keep it simple, since a complex system will not allow you to see clearly what is going on.

Why use Visual Management

In today's world, processes tend to be complex. Many involve data being stored away in computers 'hidden' until we remember to check something or we have to check because of a problem. A good system should allow you to see without the effort of 'going to find out'.

How to implement Visual Management

There are many ways to do this, but following these basic guidelines will help:

1. Make the work visible and obvious. Remove all the clutter; use the 5S tool to do this. Undertake the 1st and 2nd 'S' and mark out the area so everything has a place and there is a place for everything.

2. Post the teams performance in the area. Keep it simple, only measure 4 or 5 things based on Safety, Quality, Delivery and Cost.

3. Make it clear where non standard items such as quality rejects or defective parts should go. Make sure any abnormal items can be easily seen and are not hidden away.

Figure 2.1 Fixed Point Observation

4. Find a spot where you can stand to observe the whole area.

5. Stand on the spot. The target is for you to be able to understand any abnormalities in 10 seconds.

6. If you cannot understand something in that time, work on making that part of the process visual. Abnormalities should be clear i.e. all reject parts are easily visible and the quantity can be seen without counting.

7. Keep repeating the steps until the entire process can be understood from your spot. (If the process area is large it is permissible to have more than one spot!)

8. Check with the team that they see the same as you!

Do not fall into the trick of covering the walls with check sheets, data and posters. This will not allow you to see problems any quicker, and the sheets will just consume time to update them.

How many times do you see out of date sheets on a notice board? Proof this type of control rarely works well.

Remember one sheet used properly is better than ten that are not used at all.

By having a place for everything and everything in its place, abnormality becomes easy to see.

For instance, if we size our storage to take only the items we require, then there is no place to store any excess and the waste screams out at you!

What equipment do we use and is it clear where it is stored and where it should go back to once finished with?

Some useful Visual Management resources, techniques and methods

Andons

An andon is a device to indicate that the process has stopped for some reason.

This can be as simple as a coloured block that you place on top of your work station (just like Robert Owen).

Figure 2.2 Andon Example

Another common method is to use a series flashing lights that are connected to a central support resource. The different colours indicate the status.

In a more advanced process these lights can all be linked together into one central board to make it even more visual!

Signage

Professional signage can be a great way to create visual control. The signage can be used to indicate what should be stored in a specific location and the quantity there should be.

Colour Coding

Creating a colour code that everyone understands can have great visual impact. For example tooling can be colour coded by product type.

Floor Marking

Indicate what should go where, also walkways and traffic aisles.

Figure 2.3 Floor Marking
Example

Edging items with small pieces of tape on the floor can be an effective way to create a location for items and is relatively maintenance free.

Visual procedures

Use flow charts, text and pictures to describe the process right beside where the action takes place.

Shadow Boards

By creating a shadow around an item then it is easy to see where the item should be returned. Consider using foam cut-outs in tool cabinets to help understand if all tools are where they should be.

In conclusion

Visual control helps us to understand the status of a process or area quickly. It builds upon the disciplines of 5S and really is the supervisors 'best friend', as done well, it allows a high level of control to be easily achieved.

Try to implement the ten second rule. If you cannot understand the status of something within ten seconds, then this aspect of visual control needs to be improved.

Standard Work

One of the biggest failings in most processes is the fact that they are not repeatable.

This gives rise to a whole series of issues. Quality cannot be guaranteed if the process has variation. Operators may have difficulty keeping to the expected production 'pace' if the workload is not understood or balanced. Costs cannot be fully understood if the process time varies.

The answer is to standardise the process and develop Standard Work.

Standard Work can be defined as:

'The best combination of people and equipment whilst using the minimum amount of materials, labour, and space at any given time'

There are a number of key elements that need to be understood before a process can be standardised. These include:

- Cycle time

- Work sequence

- Takt time

Cycle Time

The Cycle Time is the time taken to complete a particular task.

Measuring cycle times, is a key component in understanding the current condition of any process.

When to measure it

It is vital that all cycle times are understood before a process can be improved. Before measuring the cycle time, ensure that the process steps are defined and all operators at least follow the prescribed steps in sequence.

Why should we measure it

There are several reasons why we need to measure cycle times.

One primary reason is to create what we call Standard Work or 'the best known way of doing something'.

The very act of measuring cycle times forces us to think about the job that is being reviewed.

Another reason for measuring cycle times is to understand how one job relates to another, so that the overall workload in a process is balanced.

How do you measure it

The simplest way to measure cycle time is by completing a Cycle Time Observation Form. As the name suggests observation is key to the process.

Figure 2.4 Cycle Time Form Example

Cycle Time Observation Form

Line / process / operator ____________ Date / time ____________ Observed by ____________

		Cycle											
	Step / Activity	1	2	3	4	5	6	7	8	9	10	Average task time	Observations / Comments / Addition points
1													
2													
3													
4													
5													
6													
7													
8													
9													
10													
	Time of one cycle												← Lowest repeatable cycle time

The process of measuring cycle time is usually best undertaken in a team of three: one to observe the process and measure the times; the second to record; and the third to perform the actual task.

The most important point to remember is that it is the process that is being timed not the person!

Once this is established follow the steps below:

1. The first thing to do is to observe the overall job from beginning to end. This allows a full understanding of what is actually going on, and all the potential problems that may exist.

2. Once we have a feel for the overall job, we are in a position to break it down into bite size chunks called elements. These are the elements that are recorded on the cycle time form. Try to breakdown the process into logical size elements. Ten elements is really the maximum. Do not break the process down into elements of just a few seconds. It will be too difficult to record.

3. Once everyone is happy start the process and using a stopwatch, record the element times. DO NOT stop the watch between individual elements as starting and stopping the watch will 'lose time'. Call out the 'split times' and work out the individual element times later.

4. The times are then recorded on the form.

5. The number of times you measure the job will depend on the time it takes. You should record the cycle a number of times, to check for consistency.

   You need to use common sense in terms of your study.

6. Once the timing of the process is complete work out the individual element times.

7. Add up the different task elements to get the overall cycle time.

8. Look for the lowest repeatable cycle time and enter this on the form. If a 'lowest' repeatable time is not clear, again use common sense. Do not use the 'fastest' time, as this will not achieve anything, since we are looking for waste and the reasons for process variation.

9. Once the form is completed, each job element should be questioned. Consider the following:
   - Is the task necessary?
   - Is the element Value Added?
   - Could the task be done a better way?
   - Could the task be combined with another task?
   - Are the tasks being done in the best sequence?
   - Are the tasks being done consistently?
   - Is there time being wasted looking for items?
   - Consider the seven wastes; is there excessive movement or transportation etc?

When you go into this level of detail, you will be amazed at the actual amount of waste that you will uncover.

Once you have identified the improvements then re-time the job with the improvements included.

Don't worry if it does not immediately show a dramatic improvement in time.

Speed will come with familiarity.

In conclusion

Measuring Cycle Time is another Lean technique that can help you identify wasted time. It is also a great first step in establishing Standard Operating Procedures.

Work Sequence

A Work Sequence is the logical sequence in which the process takes place.

Normally, in order for the work sequence to occur properly, it must meet 4 criteria:

- There must be a defined number of steps
- The sequence must be defined
- The sequence should be assigned to a single person
- The sequence must be balanced so that 'Takt time' can be achieved

Normally the work sequence is depicted as a diagram and the sequence numbers show the flow of the process. In this example, safety care points, quality checks, and standard in process stock, have been added to the diagram.

Figure 2.5 Work Sequence Example

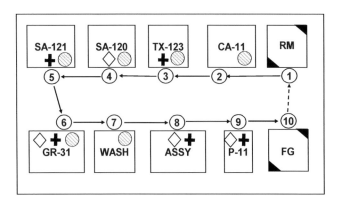

Figure 2.6 Office Work Sequence Example

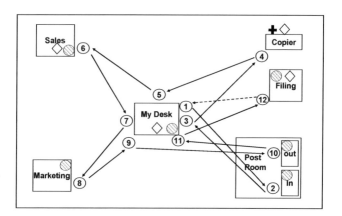

Takt Time

Takt time is one of the most important concepts to grasp in a Lean environment, since it is the principle by which the speed of the process is governed.

The word Takt is derived from the German word for beat. In the case of Lean, this refers to the pace of the process as dictated by the customer. If the customer orders 10, then 10 must be produced, not 9 or 11.

The best way to visualise this is by imagining an orchestra with the conductor at the front. He is the customer. The conductor moves his baton up and down to indicate the 'beat' of the music he requires. The musicians follow this beat, all at the same speed, completely synchronized. If he speeds up, the entire orchestra speeds up with him. As he slows down, so do the musicians.

This is the concept of Takt time. A process should adjust its output based on 'true' customer demand and not keep running at its maximum speed.

Note

"Takt time is the Beat set by the Customer...."

When and where to use it

Takt time can be calculated on virtually every task in a business environment.

It can be used in manufacturing e.g. machining parts, drilling holes etc. In administration e.g. processing orders, call centre operations etc or in a production line environment, to pace the line.

Why use it

When implemented correctly, running a process to Takt time provides many benefits. Just a few of these are:

- Since you produce only what is required by the customer, inventory is reduced

- Since the 'product' moves along the process at a given speed, bottlenecks are easily identified.

- Since problem processes are easily identified. repeat issues, like breakdowns, can be understood and fixed.

- Since the process moves at a fixed speed, work is balanced across all operators. If it is not bottlenecks will occur.

How to calculate it

A lot of confusion can be generated around Takt time calculations. The simplest way of calculating Takt time is to calculate the Takt time for the output of the process. Work from the perspective of the customer.

In order to calculate Takt time, two pieces of information are required.

- **Available Time** – this is the shift time minus any breaks, clean up time etc.

- **The Average Customer Demand** – how many does the customer *actually* require in a given period.

Work in fixed periods (days or weeks) and apply the following calculation.

Takt Time = Available time / Customer Demand

Example

A store card company receives 2,100 applications per month. And on average they work 20 days per month.

They are paid for 7.5 hours per day. They have two 15 minute coffee breaks per day – which are paid.

So the Takt time is calculated as follows:

Available time

From the 7.5 working hours 30 minutes must be deducted (for breaks).

7 hours = 420 minutes

Customer demand

2100 / 20 = 105 applications per day

$$\underline{\frac{420 \text{ minutes}}{105}} = 4 \text{ minutes}$$

So if we were processing applications to Takt time, you would expect to see an application being processed every 4 minutes. Running with a Takt time of 4 minutes means that the process is set up to deal with the customer demand as efficiently as possible.

In conclusion

Standard Work is vital in maintaining the process and training new people in a standard method of performing the operation.

Standard Work is the basis of all improvements.

As Taicchii Ohno, the kaizen guru of the Toyota Motor Company stated:

"Where there is no standard there can be no kaizen"

Kaizen is about firstly setting standards, and then continually striving to improve on those standards.

Standards are not something that should be chiselled into granite and rolled out and dusted down when the auditors are in town. They should be used on a daily basis to both train new people and confirm that experienced operators are adhering to the standard process.

Everyday Tools

In this section we shall look at a number of useful tools that can be applied in a number of situations.

These are:

- Pareto analysis

- Fishbone Diagrams

- The 5 Whys

- SWOT Analysis

- Impact Analysis

- Key Issue Identification

For all of these tools to work to the optimum, they are best applied in a team environment, since they rely on peoples' differing understanding of the issue or problem. So where ever possible, pull together a small team to apply them.

Pareto Diagrams

How to apply it

The Pareto principle is named after Italian economist Vilfredo Pareto, who observed that 80% of the wealth in Italy was owned by 20% of the population. He also noted that this 80 / 20 rule appeared to apply to a number of other situations.

Even today this rule applies to many situations and can be used to help understand data.

We can use this principle and technique to help understand where to focus efforts in situations where resources are limited and a number of problems exist.

A Pareto diagram allows data to be displayed as a chart and enables the main contributors to be easily highlighted.

1. Start by gathering the data about the problem. Use (5bar) checks sheets to do this.
   If necessary put this in place in the process for a period of time to collect real data. Make sure you have a reasonable sample size. This will make your analysis more meaningful.

   Try not to have a category heading of 'Other' because it is not definitive.

   If you find your data has this problem, add more category headings that are more meaningful. This will make things easier later.

2. Once the data is available, collate and rank the data in a similar way to the example shown in table 1.3.

Table 1.3 Example of Ranked Data

Reasons for rejects	No
Damage	17
Undersize	12
Oversize	4
Missing process	3
Rust	2
Wrong spring	1

3. Draw a bar chart showing the data. It can be useful to add a line showing the accumulated errors as a percentage. This helps in identifying the reasons that are contributing to 80% of the problems.

Figure 2.7 Pareto Chart Example

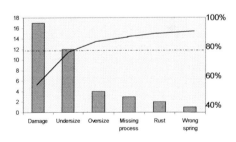

4. Review your data. Occasionally the chart will not show a clear definition of the 80/20 rule. If this is the case it maybe that you need to redefine the reasons and sub divide them or clarify them. If this is the case, re-collect the data and repeat the process.

5. Another trick is to use a 'Live Pareto'. This involves collecting the defective product, and placing them in an area in the shape of a Pareto chart. This has the added benefit of being able to examine the defective product a number of times and allows you to check that all the defects classified in one group are actually the same. It also allows you to collect other data like production times, shifts, operators etc, by marking the product. This will help you to look at the problem from another angle, without the need to start the data collection process again.

Fishbone Diagrams

When do we use it

We usually use a fishbone diagram when we are trying to get to the root cause of a problem, which has many possible causes. It can be a useful tool to use during a kaizen event to help define quality problems in a format that is easily understood.

How to apply it

Sometimes also known as a 'cause and effect diagrams', or Ishikawa diagrams, the technique involves using a diagram to help identify possible causes associated with a particular problem or 'effect'.

All possible causes are identified before narrowing down the possibilities to a small number of likely causes. These can then be addressed in a methodical manner.

1. Start by defining exactly what is to be analysed – the 'Effect'.

2. Gather a small team, since this tool is best used in the team environment as a brainstorming exercise.

3. Draw the outline Fishbone diagram.

4. Establish the Cause categories. A good starting point is to use the original 6Ms which are:

   - Material
   - Maintenance
   - Man

- Method (or Process)
- Mother Nature (Environment)

The more modern headings are:

- Materials
- Equipment
- People
- Method
- Environment

Other categories sometimes used include:

- Systems
- Management
- Policies
- Suppliers
- Customers

Try to stick to 5 categories and in the extreme use 6, but never more than 6 otherwise the process becomes too complex.

Figure 2.8 Fishbone Diagram Headings

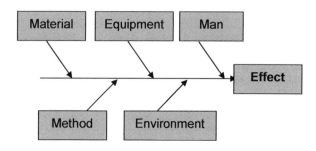

5. The team brainstorm the potential causes and add these to the branches representing the 'bones' of the fish. If you feel that a cause fits into more than one category feel free to put the cause under more than one heading. If you find that it is difficult to place a cause under a heading, this maybe a clue that the categories need refined. If this is the case, go back to step 4 and re-define the categories.

Figure 2.9 Fishbone Diagram build up

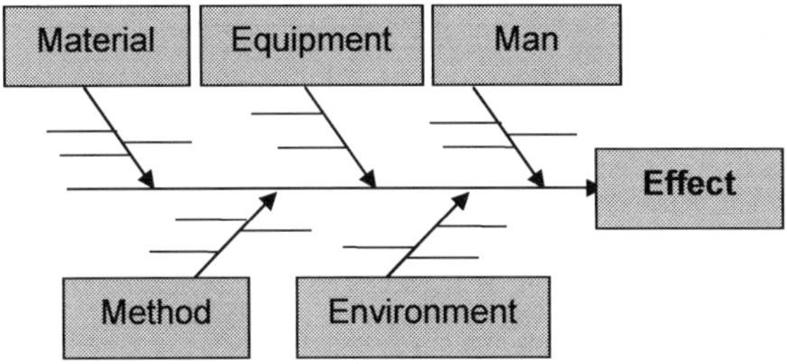

6. Be aware that the diagram can get quite busy with some 'bones' getting more heavily populated than others. This is quite normal and usually points to areas that are more influential to the problem.

7. When you have exhausted all the potential causes, the next stage is to analyse the data for root causes.

   - Look for repeat causes or a number of causes that are related.
   - Use the team to share ideas and information (this can speed up the process)
   - Use data wherever possible. Check sheets, customer surveys, process maps, breakdown reports plus any number of others are valuable sources of data. Use Pareto Analysis to correlate the data further.

- Use the data to both dismiss and confirm potential root causes.
- Keep a record of why you reach your conclusions.

8. Once you have narrowed down the causes in to a manageable number, test your theories. Again use data. If possible simulate potential root causes and measure the effect. Again eliminate any causes that you can.

9. When the process has been exhausted and you have the root cause, put a temporary counter measure in place and analyse the effect. If the problem does not reoccur, the root cause has been found, and a more permanent solution can be put in place.

In conclusion

Fishbone diagrams are a quick and easy improvement tool that can help you identify root causes to sometimes quite difficult problems. It's a great way of collating group input in a pictorial form, which everyone can understand.

The 5 Whys

How to apply it

The concept of this technique is very simple. Keep asking why until the root cause of a particular problem had been identified.

Although this technique is called '5 Why's', in practice you ask the question 'Why?' any number of times until the process is exhausted and the root cause has been uncovered. The norm is 5 times, hence the name.

Figure 3.0 Example of 5 Whys

Why is there a high scrap rate of part 123?
Because some parts are rusty

Why are the parts rusty?
Because the parts are getting wet

Why are the parts getting wet?
Because the storage boxes are wet

Why are the storage boxes wet?
Because they are stored outside

Why are they stored outside?
Because the rack is full

Why is the rack full?
Because we have too much stock

The process in this example could be continued to understand why too much stock had been manufactured and uncover the real root cause.

It is important to make sure you stay 'narrow and deep' down an avenue and do not deviate from the original problem.

SWOT Analysis

How to apply it

SWOT Analysis is a graphical method of summarising a particular department, area, process or part, looking at its strengths, weaknesses, opportunities and threats.

1. Start by defining exactly what is to be analysed.

2. Gather a small team, since this tool is best used in the team environment as a brainstorming exercise.

3. Systematically brainstorm the 4 areas one by one:

   - **Strengths.** The characteristics of performance or behaviour that is strong

   - **Weaknesses**. The characteristics which are weakest

   - **Opportunities.** Any chances that exist to improve, grow or strengthen the process

   - **Threats.** Risks to the stability of the process. Things that could be detrimental to performance

4. Use a flip chart or similar to produce a chart similar to the example in Figure 3.1 on the next page.

Figure 3.1 Example of a SWOT Chart

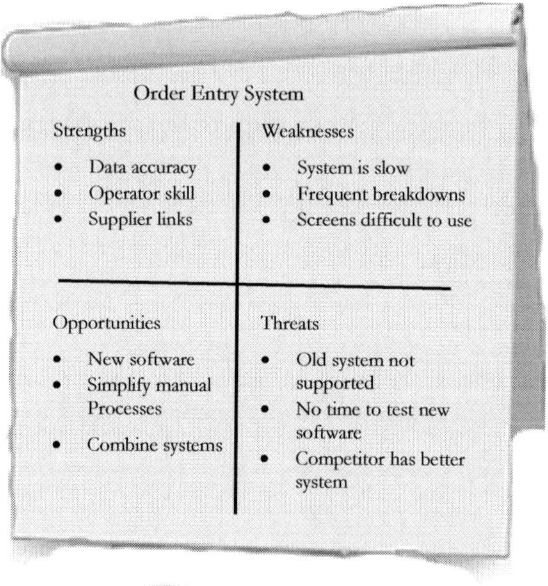

Order Entry System

Strengths	Weaknesses
• Data accuracy	• System is slow
• Operator skill	• Frequent breakdowns
• Supplier links	• Screens difficult to use
Opportunities	**Threats**
• New software	• Old system not supported
• Simplify manual Processes	• No time to test new software
• Combine systems	• Competitor has better system

5. When the brainstorming is complete, review the points one by one as a group, and rank the factors by importance or impact, either by discussion or voting.

Impact Analysis

Impact Analysis is a useful technique to prioritise a list of potential improvement ideas.

It helps to review a group of potential actions in terms of their impact and ease of implementation.

When to use it

Primarily it works best for a team of between 8-12 people who are working on some sort of improvement activity together. It is best to have an independent facilitator to lead the activity. This technique can be used at anytime once you have a set of improvement actions to prioritise.

Why use it

The main reason we use Impact Analysis is to take a number of potential improvement actions to group them into four meaningful sub groups.

1. Those actions that will have a big impact on our objectives and are fairly easy to implement.

2. Those actions that will only have a small impact on our objectives and are fairly easy to implement.

3. Those actions that will have a big impact on our objectives but are more difficult to implement

4. Those actions that will only have a small impact on our objectives and are more difficult to implement.

How do I use it

Preparation

1. Equipment/Facilities

    You will need the following to create an Impact Analysis Chart

    *   Sticky notes
    *   Markers
    *   Flip chart paper
    *   Masking tape
    *   A room with large free wall space.

2. Team Members/Facilitator

    The team should be made up with people who understand the implications of the improvement actions being considered.

It is always useful to have an experienced facilitator to lead this activity.

3. Create this chart on flip chart paper::

Figure 3.2 Impact Analysis Chart

•HIGH IMPACT •LOW DIFFICULTY	•HIGH IMPACT •HIGH DIFFICULTY
•LOW IMPACT •LOW DIFFICULTY	•LOW IMPACT •HIGH DIFFICULTY

4. Team members then write down potential improvement ideas onto sticky notes around the objective that has been set for them.

5. Team members then critique ideas and decide which category of the chart they fall under.

Top left quadrant:	High Impact / Low Difficulty
Bottom left quadrant:	Low Impact / Low Difficulty
Top right quadrant:	High Impact / High Difficulty
Bottom right quadrant:	Low Impact /High Difficulty

The following questions should be considered for each idea:

- Will the idea have a high or low impact on the objectives we are working on?

- Will the idea be easy or difficult to implement.

6. Each sticky note in turn is added to the appropriate quadrant grid on the chart.

7. It's usually best to work on high impact low difficulty ideas first and then low impact low difficulty items next.

The High Impact / High Difficulty ideas can make the basis for a longer term improvement plan.

Low Impact / High Difficulty items may not even be considered depending on resources.

In conclusion

Impact Analysis can help you prioritise potential improvement actions very quickly.

It helps to review a group of potential actions in terms of their impact and ease of implementation.

Key Issue Identification

Key Issue Identification is a technique for getting consensus around the important issues that a group are facing using a lightning fast process.

It is a great way to get people thinking about the current issues and challenges facing them in a very short space of time.

Who should be involved

Basically, anyone who has experience of, and a vested interest in, resolving the issue that you are currently looking at.

When should you use it

This technique can be used at any time to drill down to the vital areas that are affecting performance.

It is a great way to get a common list of key issues at the beginning of a kaizen blitz week. (Or any reasonable sized project)

It can also be used at an operational team level to let people share their current issues in a constructive way. (Rather than the usual whinging session)

Where should you do it

You can do this anywhere.
The only real requirement for creating a key issue chart is a large piece of wall and enough surrounding space to allow people to move sticky notes about.

Why use it

It is very fast.

This technique allows you to very quickly highlight a lot of facts about a particular issue, and then drill down to the key issues that are affecting the groups' performance.

How do you do it

Preparation

1. Equipment/Facilities

   You will need the following to create an Key Issues Chart

   - Sticky notes
   - Markers
   - Flip chart paper
   - Sticky Tack
   - Dot labels (3 colours)
   - A room with large free wall space.

2. Team Members/Facilitator

   The team should be made up with people who are knowledgeable about the issue being reviewed. (typically 8-12 people)

   It is always useful to have an experienced facilitator to lead the activity who is neutral to the process.

3. Timing

   This depends on the size of the task .It can take anything from an hour, up to a full day depending on the level of detail you go into.

4. Creating the key issue chart
   Join four pieces of flip chart paper together and sticky tack them to the wall. Experience will tell you how big this backdrop should be. Using flip chart paper allows you to add or take away as required, and gives the sticky notes a surface to adhere to.

5. Agree in the group the business issue that you want to explore together. This should be written up on a flipchart so that everyone can see it and agree it. The more precise you can be with the statement, the better you will find the process. e.g. Write up on the flip chart...
   "What is preventing us from turning around client applications in less than 1 working day?"

6. There should be group consensus that the statement is a meaningful articulation of the business issue affecting the team. We should rework the statement till everyone is happy with it.

7. Give everyone in the group at least seven sticky notes each. Each person should then write down facts about the statement. There should only be one fact per sticky note.

   The sticky notes should be printed legibly as everyone has to be able to read them. We are looking for at least seven facts from each person.

   People should only write down facts in a reporting style and not in an affective style. e.g. "The last 3 applications I received had missing contact details". Not, "The application forms are rubbish".

8. Each person in the group then reads out their facts from the sticky notes, to ensure understanding.
   They should be challenged by other members of the group if they are not facts or not written in a reporting style. (They should be re-written until acceptable)

Once all of their sticky notes are explained they should then place the sticky notes on the blank chart on the wall. This process should continue until all of the group have their sticky notes on the wall.

9. In silence ... yes in silence, the group arranges the sticky notes on the wall with "like facts".

    Why in silence? Experience shows that if you are allowed to speak at this stage one or two individuals can dominate proceedings. Doing it in silence gives better grouping.

    At the end of this stage one should end up with several groups of like facts, clustered together on the wall.

10. The group should then take the groups of facts and write a summary sticky note (in a different colour) for each group.

11. Voting.
    Again in silence each person should vote for their top 3 issues as detailed on the summary sticky note, using different coloured dot labels.

    Assign a score to each dot

    e.g. red dot =3, blue dot=2, green dot = 1

    Each person only gets 3 dots (3 votes)

    Points make prizes...

    The summary sticky note they feel is the biggest issue should get the biggest score (i.e. they should stick a red dot on that sticky note)

12. Once everyone has voted, total up all of the scores on the sticky notes. Usually two or three issues come out as clear favourites. Don't get too immersed in the scores! This is a quick and efficient way of identifying the top few issues affecting performance.

13. Now tidy up the chart by trying to draw relationships between the different summary issues.

In Conclusion

Key issue identification helps one understand the collective current issues very quickly, and can prove a sound basis from which to make improvements.

By using and insisting on 'facts' about a particular issue it focuses directly on the key issues that need to be addressed.

It's a great technique for galvanising a group quickly on a particular business issue.

Performance Tracking

One thing to be considered when you are working in a Lean environment is tracking performance.

As improvements are made to the process you must be able to measure their effectiveness. Data collected on performance will also help in communication and will take the 'emotion' out of conversations. It helps identify abnormalities, and allows you to see the issues more clearly.

What ever data is tracked it must be:

- Visual
- Inclusive of targets
- Clear and easily understood
- Reviewed and acted upon daily

Many organisations collect data, but simple do not use the data effectively.

One of the best ways of doing overcoming this issue this is by using an SQDC board.

SQDC Boards

SQDC boards are a vital part of the visual process. Their purpose is to provide a snap shot of the status of a department, production line or a process. Normally the SQDC boards are aligned to teams since they should be used at team level to help understand team performance.

SQDC stands for **S**afety, **Q**uality, **D**elivery, and **C**ost. These are generally considered the four areas of performance that should be measured by any team.

When and where to use SQDC boards

SQDC boards are normally sited in a team area and should be used to focus on of all the team's improvements efforts.

Why Use SQDC Boards

One of the biggest problems of communication within an organisation is being able to provide real time information on performance down to team level. Many companies struggle to get sufficient detail, and then communication becomes watered down and almost useless from the point of view of understanding individual team performance.

SQDC boards are used to overcome this issue.

The key is for the team to collect and analyse its own data to a large degree. The board should be considered as a 'local information centre' and not be filled with high level corporate information.

Using SQDC boards correctly, will allow more detailed information of an areas performance to be collected. This can then be analysed by the local team, and agree corrective actions to be put in place for any issues that have been uncovered.

How to used SQDC boards.

The actual design of the board will vary from company to company. In some companies they are called SQDCM boards with the last column displaying data on Morale, such as Absenteeism. Whatever design is used, ensure the board is located locally to the team and there is sufficient space around it for the team to meet.

When in place, all team meetings should be held around the board.

The example on the next page, (Figure 3.3) illustrates that the layout is set out in a specific manner. The four headings are across the board and each column has information that includes:

- Recent data. How did we do today?

- Trend data: Performance year to date

- Pareto Chart: Most common reasons for problems

- Actions: How, who and when will the problems be fixed.

Figure 3.3 SQDC Board example

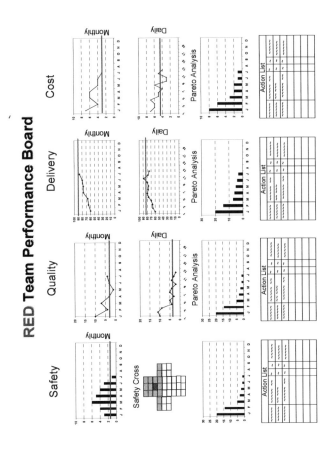

In conclusion

SQDC Boards are the most effective way of tracking a team's performance as long as the data is relevant and acted upon.

People generally respond well to the knowledge of how well they are performing. It helps team bonding when there is an understanding of the problems and the action plan to solve them.

Make sure data is collected using an easy method. Use the KIS principle (Keep It Simple)

Do not try to fix everything at once. Focus on the big issues indicated by the Pareto Chart.

Spread the load, work as a team and ask for help from other areas or departments, if it is needed.

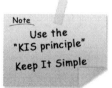

Glossary of Terms

This final section covers a Glossary of Terms often used to describe different aspects of 'Lean Thinking'.

5S: A process and method for creating and maintaining an organized, clean and high performance workplace. The 5S's are taken originally from 5 Japanese words, Seiri, Seiton, Seiso, Seiketsu and Shitsuke.

5 Whys: The 5 why's typically refer to the practice of asking, 5 times, why the failure has occurred in order to get to the root cause of the problem. There can be more than one cause to a problem. In an organizational context, generally root cause analysis is carried out by a team of people related to the problem. No special technique is required.

Abnormality management: The ability to see and respond to an abnormality (any violation of standard operations) in a timely manner.

Andon: A signal, light, bell, music alarm, triggered by an operator confronted with a non-standard condition: tool failure; machine failure; bad part; lack of parts; cannot keep up; error needs correction etc. Andons can also be used to signal for assistance to help to prevent the process stopping.

Autonomation: English translation of Jidoka. Imparting human intelligence to a machine so that it automatically stops when a problem arises.

Batch: A run of like products/parts through a process (number of product/parts run between product changeover).

Brainstorming: Consensus building about a problem or issue using group discussion. All ideas are listed without comment or regard to feasibility.

Buffer: Typically used to describe the amount of inventory or queue in front of an operation.

Capacity: The amount of production over a given time period.

Cellular manufacturing: An alignment of machines in correct process sequence, where operators remain within the cell and materials are presented to them from outside.

Cycle Time: The time to complete a specific process. This must not be confused with Lead time which normally includes waiting time cumulated before, during and after the process and is a product of WIP.

Demand: The amount of product a customer requires over time, such as: daily, weekly, monthly etc.

Downtime: Non–productive time generally due to equipment stoppage, lack of materials, or lack of operators – generally refers to machine breakdowns

Elemental time: Time allotted to a specific operational step, within standard work.

External Setup: a setup that can be done while a machine or process is in operation. This type of set up does not delay production.

Finished Goods: Completed product ready for shipment to the customer.

Fire fighting: An expression used to describe the process of performing emergency fixes to problems.

Forecast: The prediction of demand over a given time period based on input from Sales and Marketing, and historical trends.

Heijunka: The leveling of variety and/or volume of items produced at a process over a period of time. Used to avoid excessive batching of product types and/or volume fluctuations.

Internal Setup: Setup that must be performed while the machine or process is not operating. Production cannot take place during this time.

Jidoka: Also known as automonation. The imparting of human intelligence to a machine so that it automatically stops when a problem arises.

Just in Time (JIT): Defined as 'giving the customer what they want, when they need it, with the required Quality, whilst using the minimum amount of resources (labour, space, equipment and WIP i.e. lowest cost).

Kaizen: (Translated 'Kai' – Change, 'Zen' – Good,) A continuous improvement vehicle for driving quick hit value by implementing "Do now" solutions through waste elimination

Kanban: Japanese word for signal. It is used in a pull system to signal when production is to start, and can take a number of forms (e.g., cards, boards, lights, bins, etc).

Lead Time: The total time taken to fulfil an order.

Lean Production: A manufacturing strategy that uses less of everything compared to traditional manufacturing. The focus is on eliminating waste or Non Value Added activities within a process.

Muda: Any activity that adds to cost without adding to value of the product.

Mura: Variations in process quality, cost and delivery

Muri: Unreasonableness; demand exceeds capacity.

Non Value Add: Any activity that does not add form, feature or function to the product. Non Value Added activities include transportation, storage, inventory/buffers, handling, queues, machine repairs, etc.

One piece flow: A manufacturing philosophy which supports the movement of product from one workstation to the next, one piece at a time, without allowing inventory to build up in between.

Operator Cycle time (OCT) : The time it takes for the operator to complete a predetermined sequence of operations, inclusive of loading and unloading, exclusive of time spent waiting.

Pacemaker: A technique for pacing a process to Takt time

Pareto chart: A graphical technique used to quantify problems so that effort can be expended in fixing the "vital few" causes, as opposed to the 'trivial many'.

Pareto principle: 80% of the trouble comes from 20% of the problems (i.e., the vital few problems).

Point Kaizen: An improvement activity intensely directed at a single workstation, performed quickly by two or three specialists. Typically follows a full-blown kaizen event.

Point of Use Storage: Term for the storing of material only at the place that it will be consumed. This help eliminates warehousing and extra Non Value Add handling.

Poke Yoke: Japanese term meaning error prevention. Ideally this is an engineered method or solution which makes it very difficult or impossible to produce a defective part. It can also be applied in the manufacturing process in a number of ways i.e. only one type of bolt used within a specific workstation to prevent wrong part usage.

Problem solving: The process of determining the cause from a symptom and then choosing an action to improve a process or product.

Process flow diagram (chart): Path of steps of work used to produce a product or perform a function.

Processing Time: Time required performing a process on an individual part.

Production Smoothing: A method of production scheduling that, over a period of time, takes the fluctuation of customer demand out of manufacturing. Producing every part, every day.

Pull System: Process that authorises production as inventory is consumed. A pull system directly responds to plant changes, but must be forced to accommodate customer due dates. The Toyota Production System is an example of a classic pull system.

Push System: Process that schedules production based on demand. A push system directly accommodates customer due dates, but must be forced to respond to plant changes. MRP is an example of a classic push system.

Red Tagging: Term used within the 5's process to identify material that is no longer required at a specific workstation or place. Following the red tagging process the items should be removed in order that the clutter is removed and the workstation becomes more efficient.

Rework: Non Value Add work performed to correct a defect that has occurred.

Routing: A defined path a product takes as it is moved from operation to operation throughout a process to achieve a final product.

Safety Stock: The amount of inventory needed to compensate for variation (i.e. demand, quality, and supplier delivery).

Setup: The process of changing from producing one product type to a different type. Contains both internal and external elements.

Setup Time: The length of time taken from the last good product of a production run, to the first good product(s) of the next production run. This should include any inspection time that is required to confirm the initial product following the changeover.

Six Sigma: Started in Motorola, it is a technique that focuses on improving processes by reducing variability. Six Sigma refers to a quality level of 3.4 defects per million opportunities.

SMED: An Acronym that stands for **S**ingle **M**inute **E**xchange of **D**ies. The process that allows a person to reduce the time to change a production process over from making one part or product to another part or product. In the best companies the process must take less than ten minutes (hence single minute).

Standard Operation; The best combination of people and machines utilizing the minimum amount of labour, space, inventory and equipment.

Standard Work in Process: (SWIP) Minimum material required to complete one cycle of operator work without delay.

Supermarket: A shop floor, line-side location where parts are sorted and made ready for presentation to operators.

Takt Time: The required rate of production needed to meet 'true' customer demand.
Calculated by dividing the total net daily operating time by the total daily customer demand.

Total Preventative Maintenance: (TPM) A proactive approach to equipment maintenance involving maintenance personnel and operators focusing on maintaining reliable equipment, eliminating breakdowns, and eliminating equipment related defects.

Value Add Activities: Any effort or operation that transforms a product closer to what the customer ordered.

Value Stream: All activities, both Value Added and Non Value Added, required to bring a product group or service from order to the hands of the customer,

Value Stream Map: (or Value Chain Map) A visual picture of how material and information flows from suppliers, through manufacturing, to the customer. It includes calculations of total cycle time and Value Added Time. Typically written for the current state of the value chain and the future, to indicate where the business is going.

Waste: Anything that does not add value to the final product or service, in the eyes of the customer. An activity the customer wouldn't want to pay for if they knew it was happening. Normally classified into 7 categories.

1. Defects
2. Over Production
3. Inventory
4. Over Processing
5. Motion
6. Waiting
7. Transportation

Work In Process: (WIP) Materials that have been released into production for processing but have not been completed as finished goods.

Work Sequence: The correct steps the operator takes, in the order in which they should be taken.

Notes

Notes

3489431R00056

Printed in Great Britain
by Amazon.co.uk, Ltd.,
Marston Gate.